blue skies & other irving berlin songs

arranged by Brent Edstrom

T0066483

contents

ISBN 978-1-4950-7569-8

Blue Skies™ is a trademark of the Estate of Irving Berlin

Irving Berlin logo® and Irving Berlin Music Company® are registered trademarks of the Estate of Irving Berlin

Irving Berlin Music Company®
www.irvingberlin.com

EXCLUSIVELY DISTRIBUTED BY

Visit Hal Leonard Online at
www.halleonard.com

Contact us:
Hal Leonard
7777 West Bluemound Road
Milwaukee, WI 53213
Email: info@halleonard.com

In Europe, contact:
Hal Leonard Europe Limited
42 Wigmore Street
Marylebone, London, W1U 2RN
Email: info@halleonardeurope.com

In Australia, contact:
Hal Leonard Australia Pty. Ltd.
4 Lentara Court
Cheltenham, Victoria, 3192 Australia
Email: info@halleonard.com.au

ALL BY MYSELF

Words and Music by
IRVING BERLIN

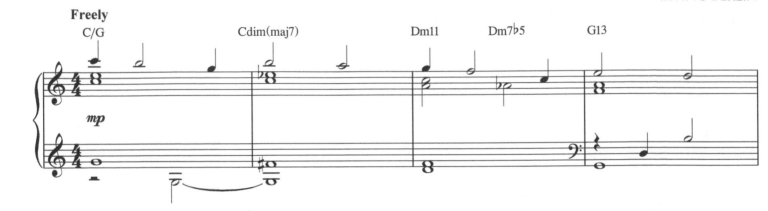

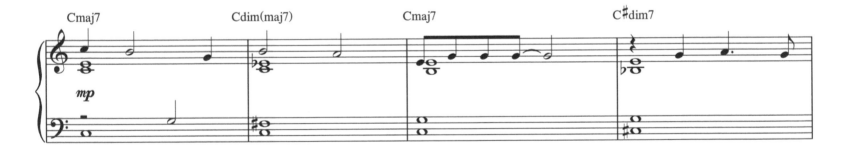

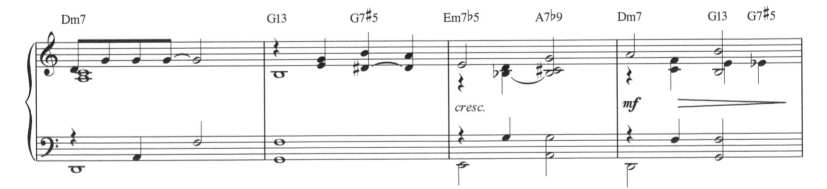

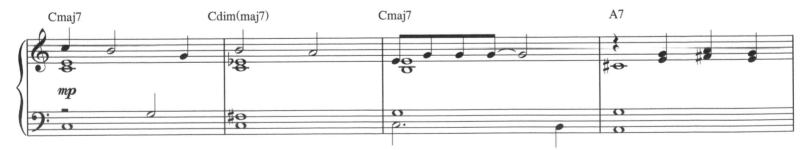

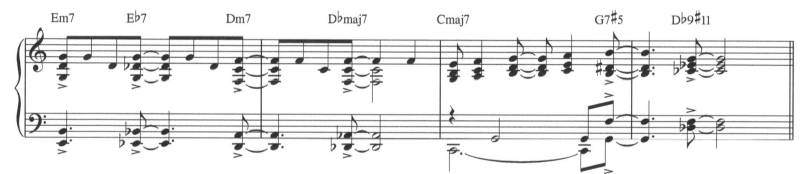

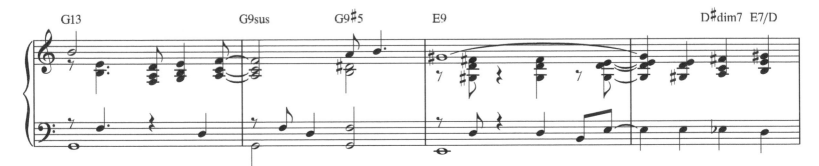

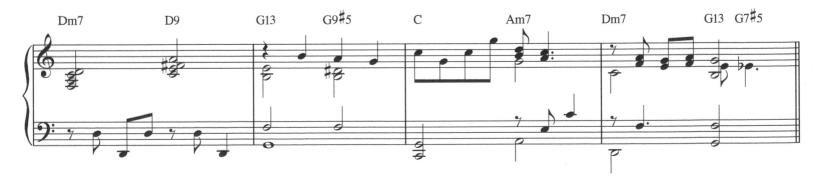

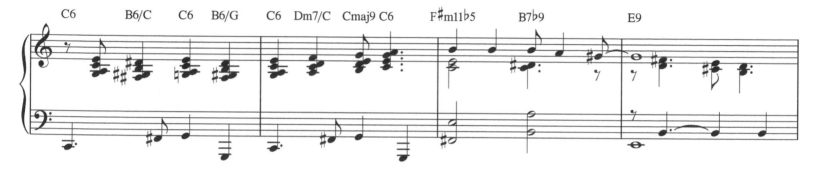

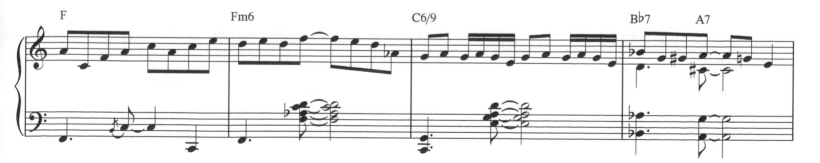

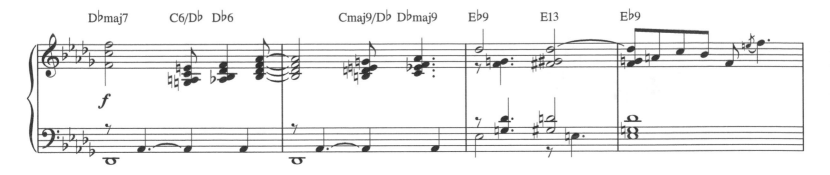

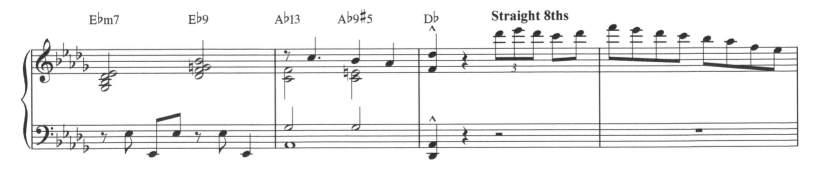

BLUE SKIES
from BETSY

Words and Music by
IRVING BERLIN

Moderate Swing

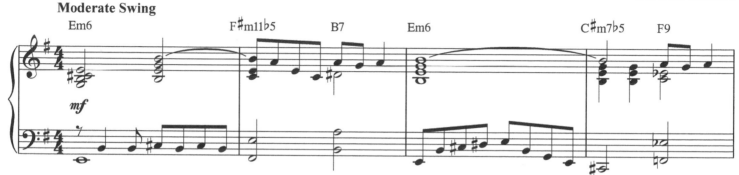

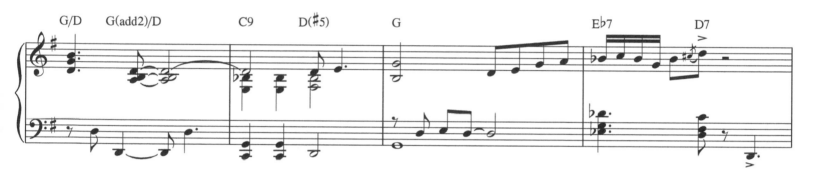

Whimsically, straight 8ths

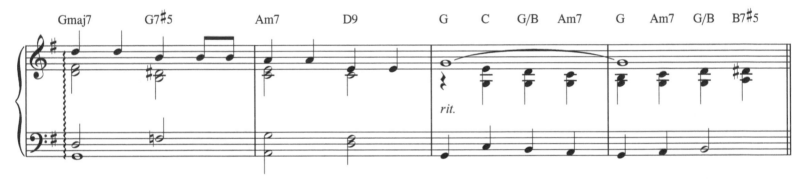

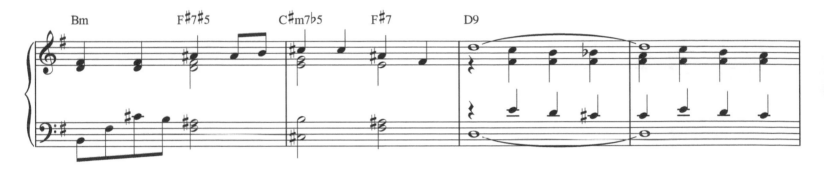

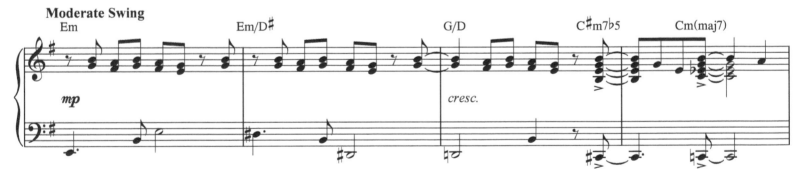

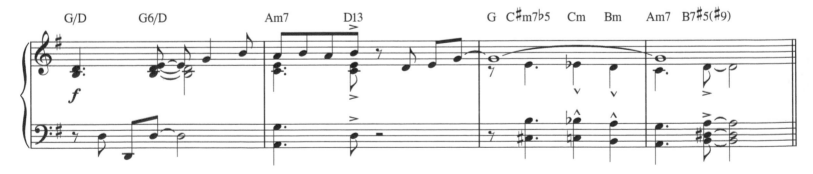

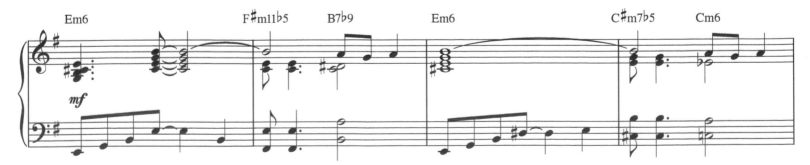

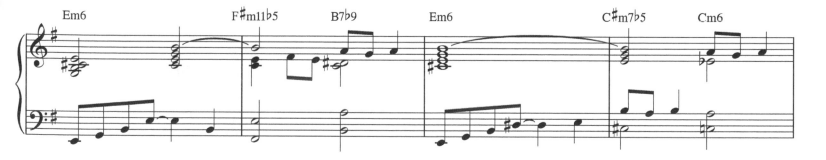

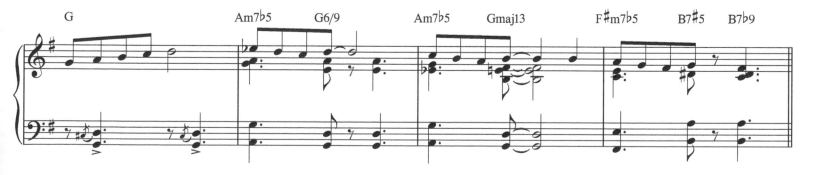

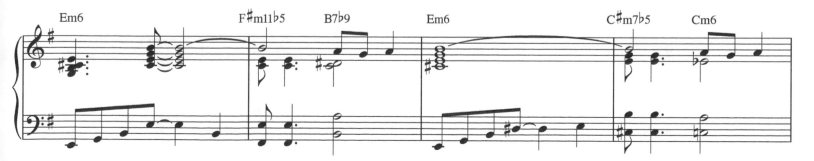

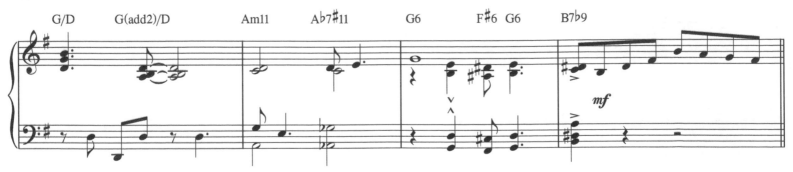

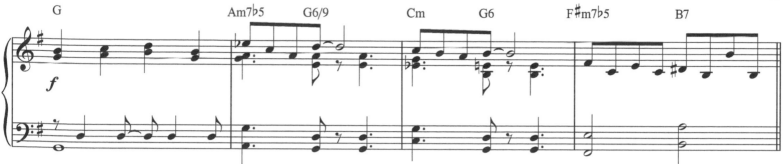

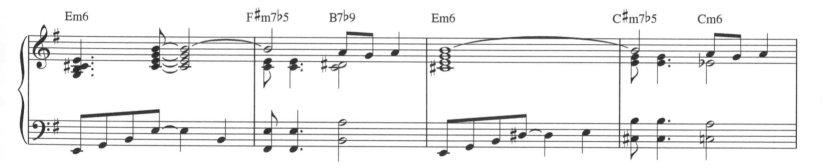

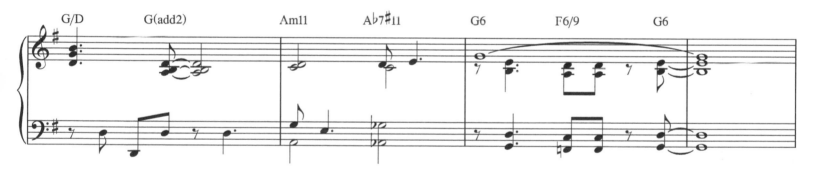

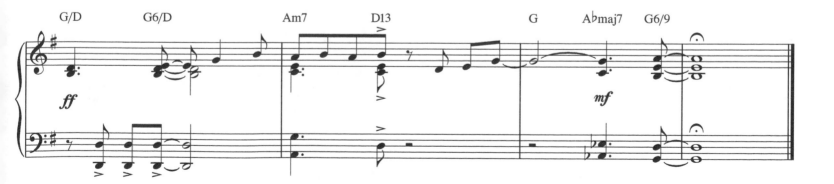

ALWAYS

Words and Music by
IRVING BERLIN

Moderate Swing

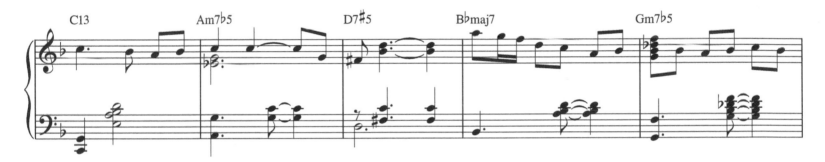

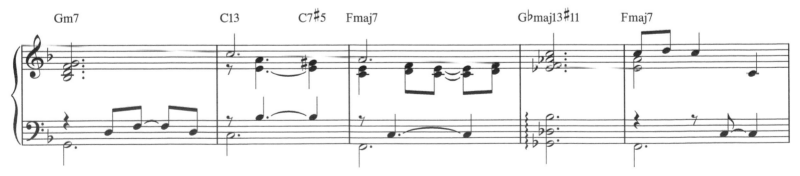

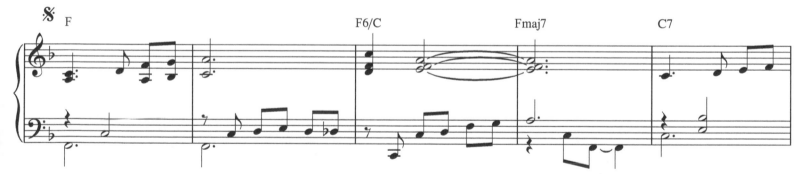

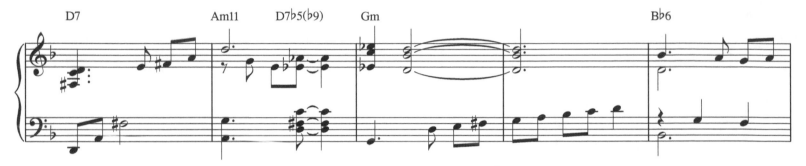

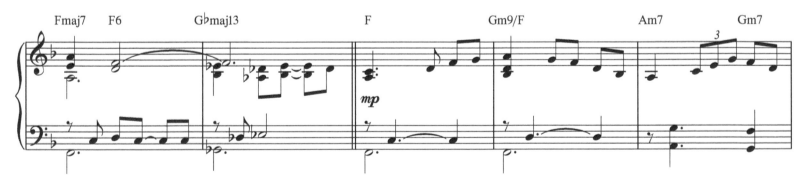

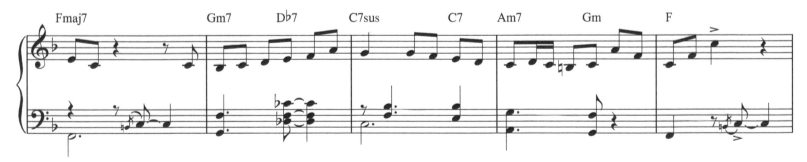

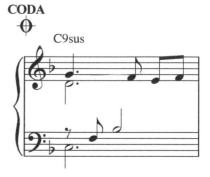

D.S. al Coda

CODA

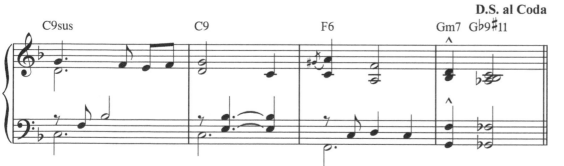

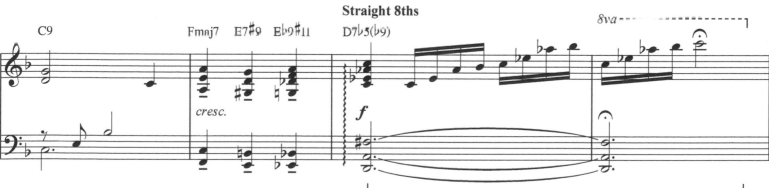

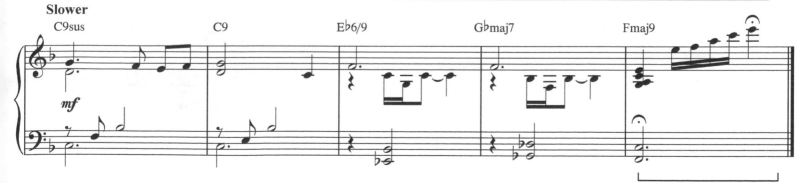

BE CAREFUL, IT'S MY HEART

from HOLIDAY INN

Words and Music by
IRVING BERLIN

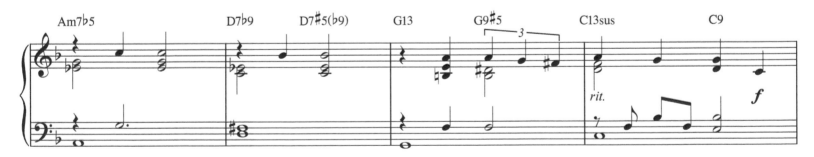

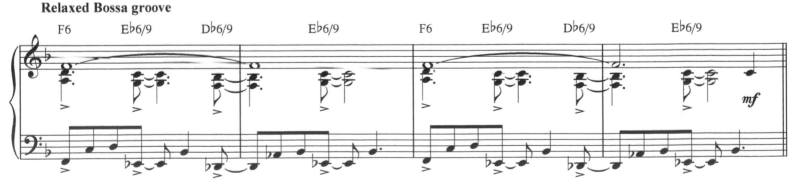

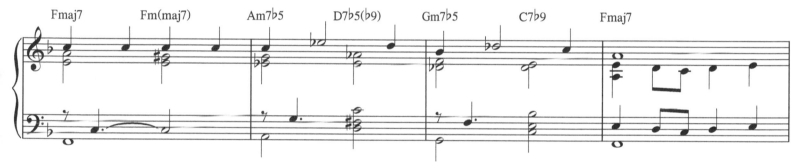

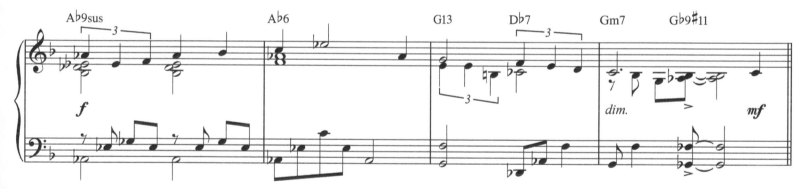

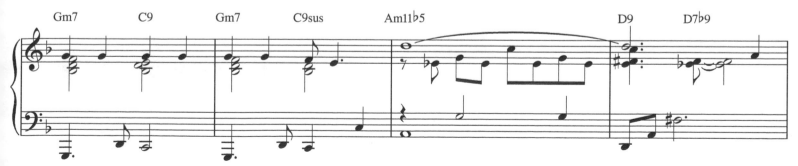

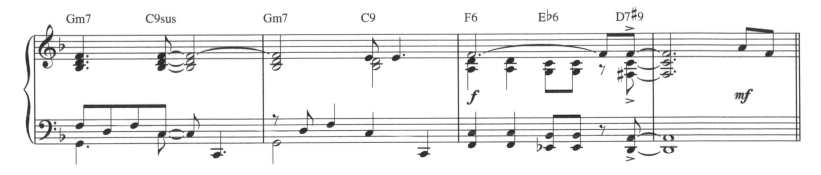

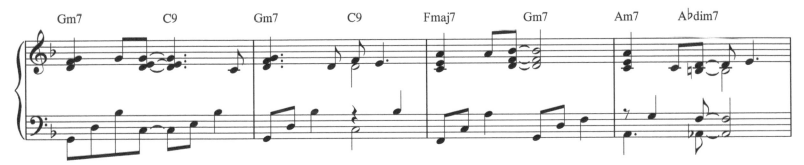

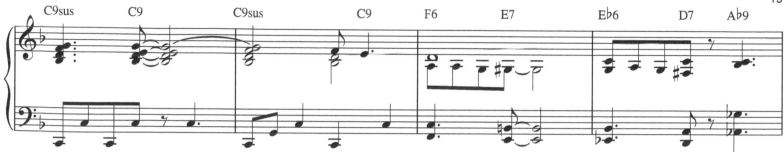

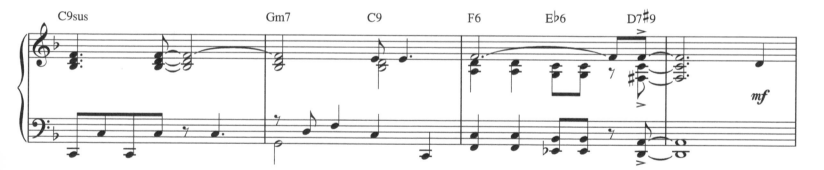

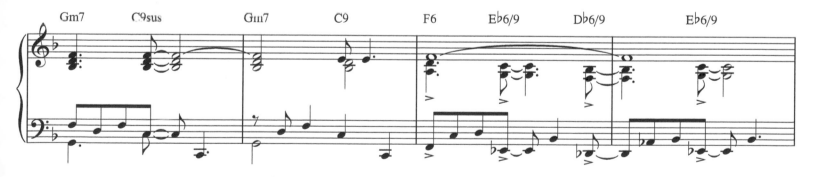

CHANGE PARTNERS
from the RKO Radio Motion Picture CAREFREE

Words and Music by
IRVING BERLIN

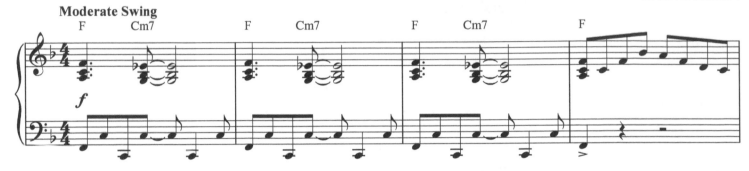

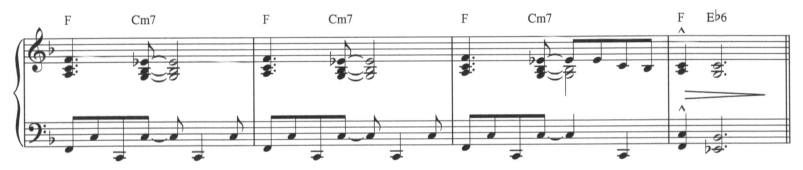

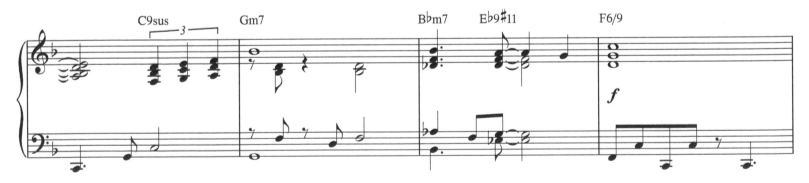

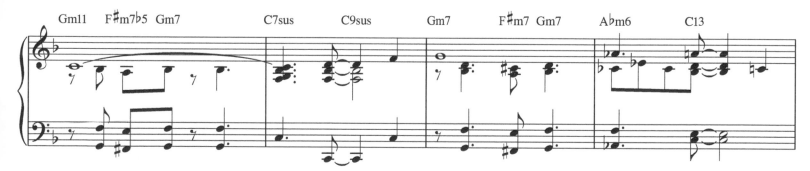

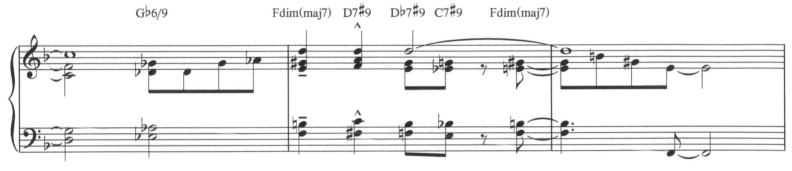

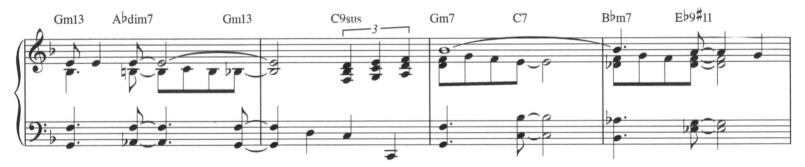

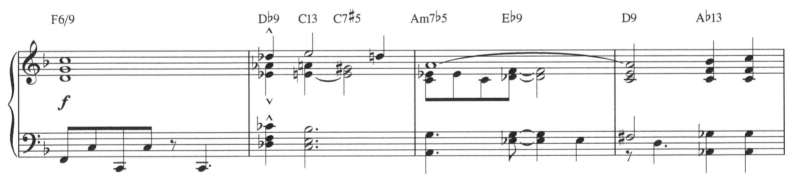

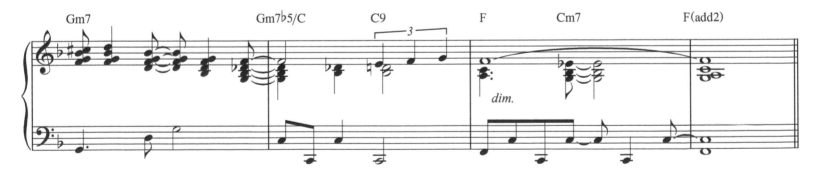

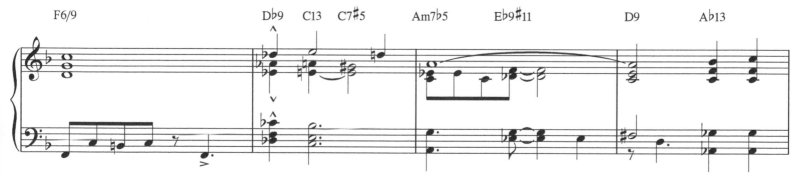

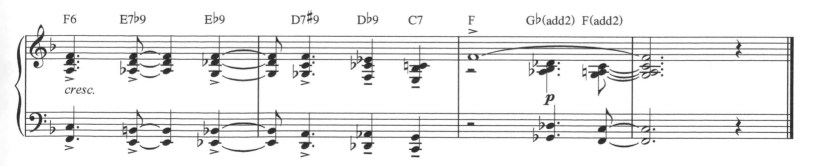

CHEEK TO CHEEK
from the RKO Radio Motion Picture TOP HAT

Words and Music by
IRVING BERLIN

Bright Swing

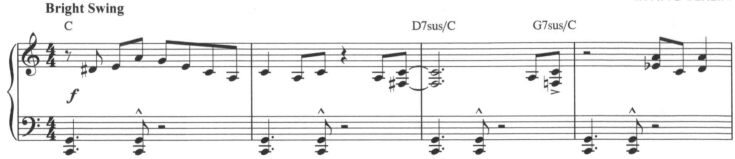

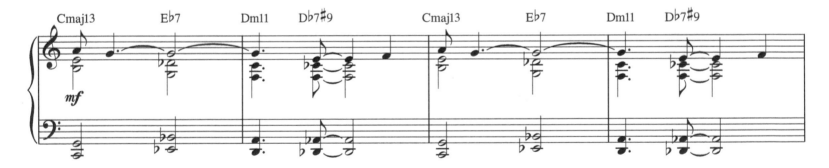

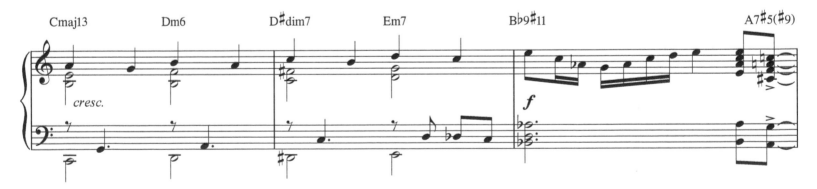

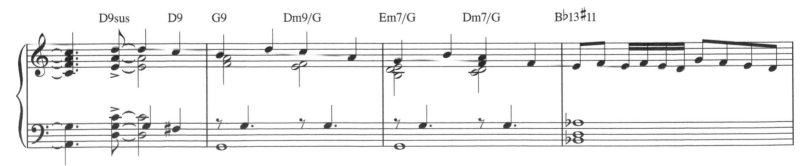

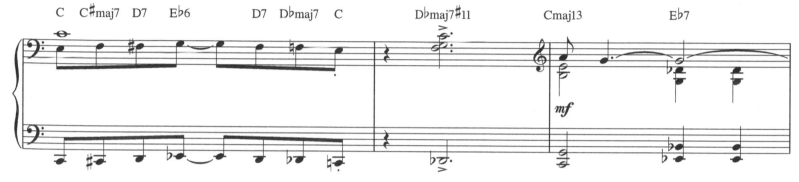

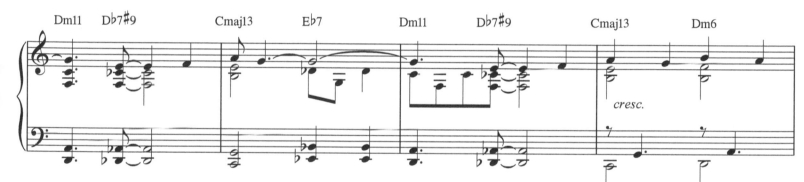

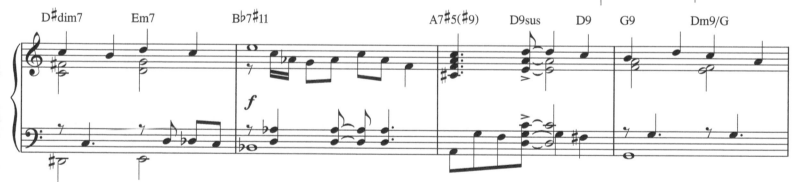

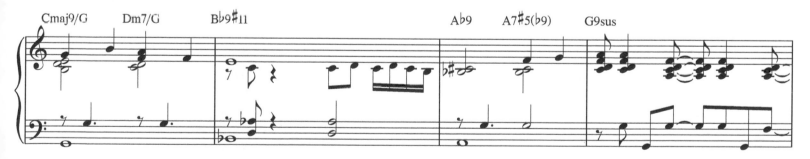

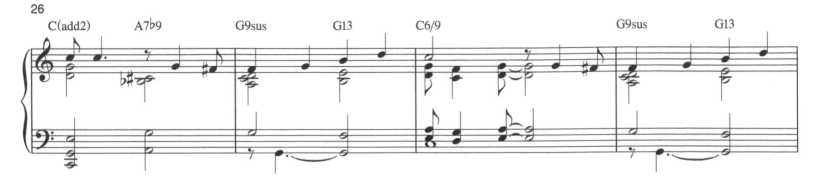

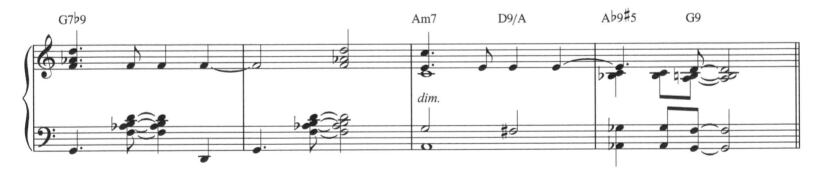

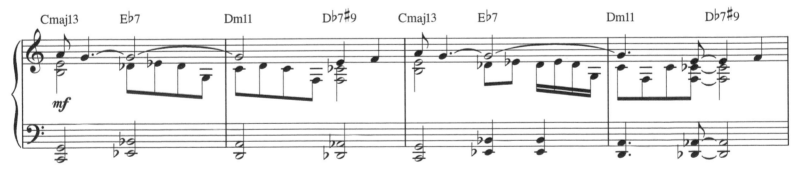

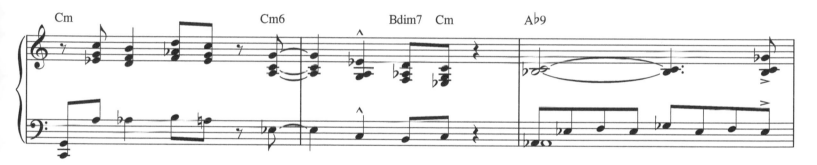

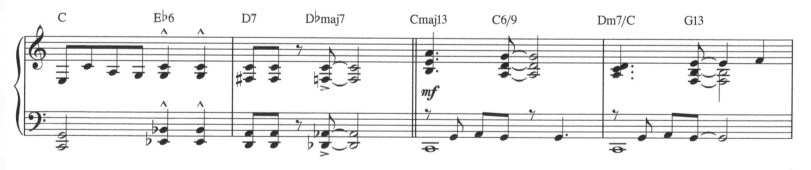

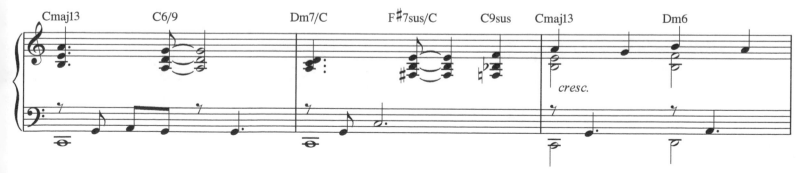

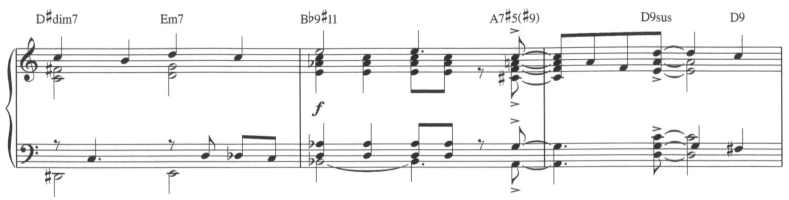

I'VE GOT MY LOVE TO KEEP ME WARM

from the 20th Century Fox Motion Picture ON THE AVENUE

Words and Music by
IRVING BERLIN

Bright jump tempo

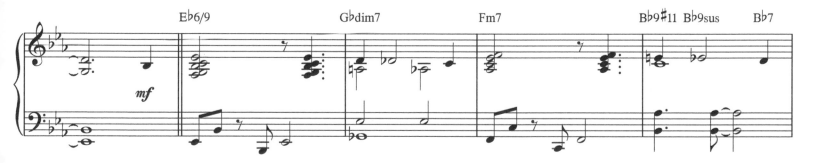

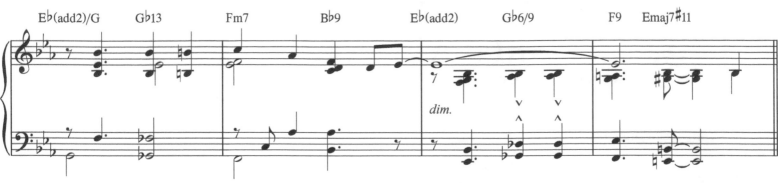

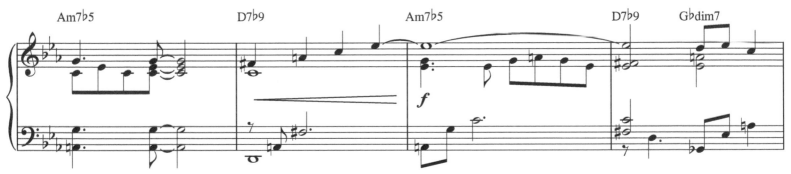

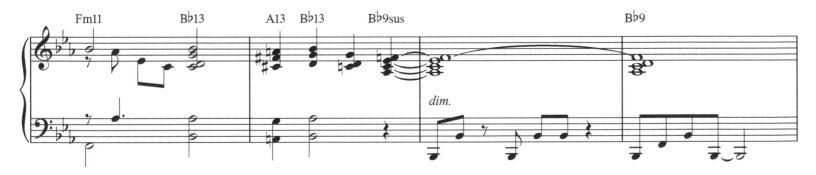

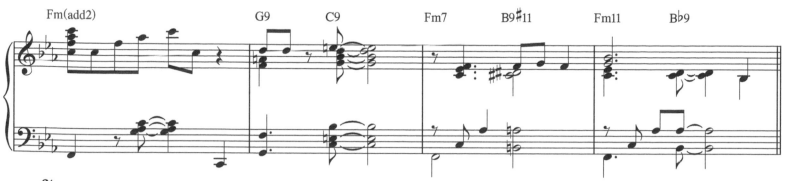

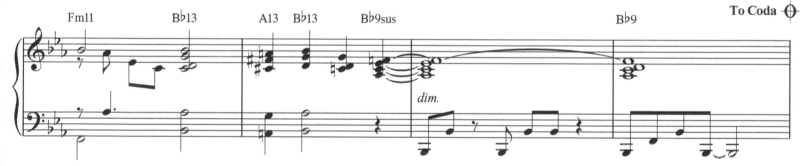

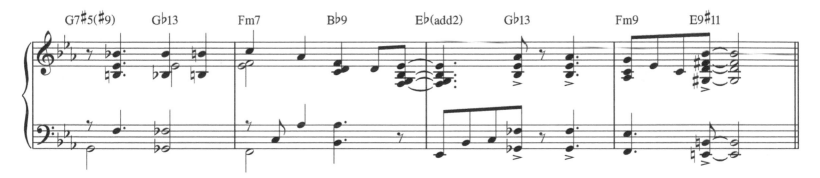

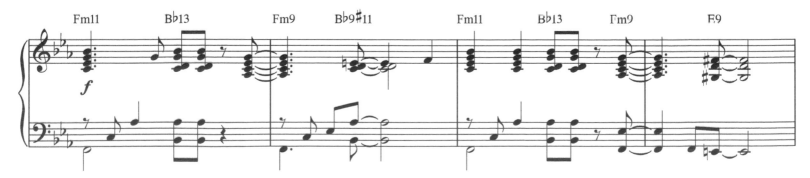

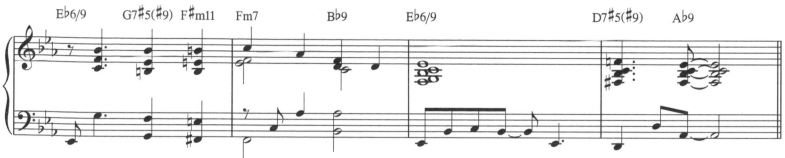

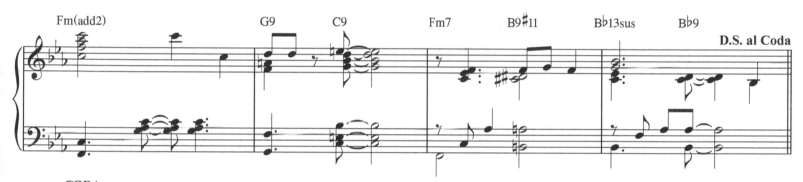

HOW DEEP IS THE OCEAN
(How High Is the Sky)

Words and Music by
IRVING BERLIN

Moderately slow Swing

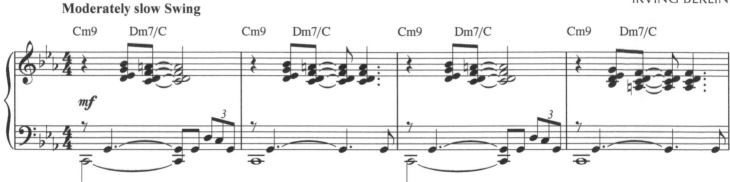

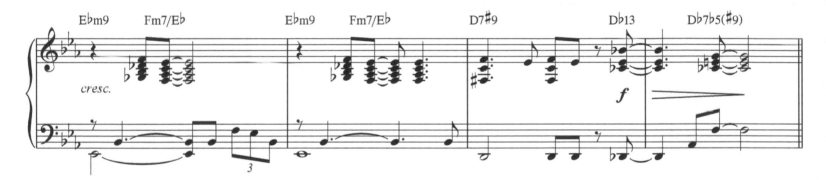

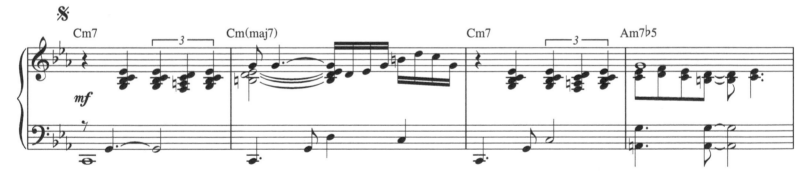

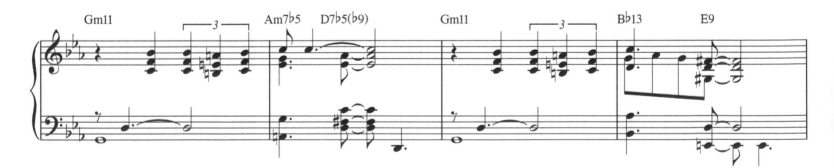

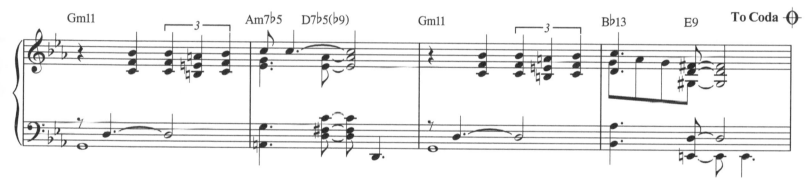

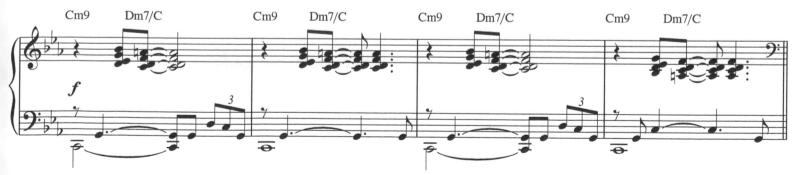

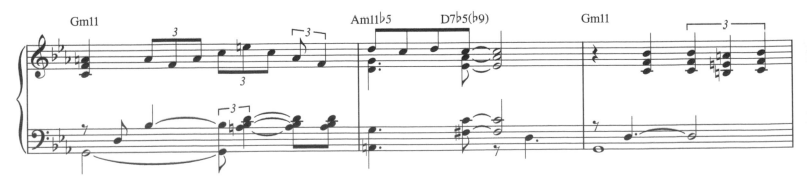

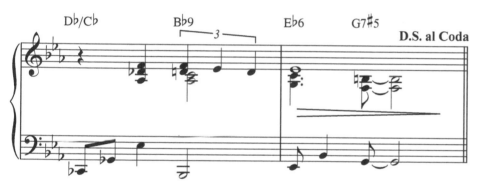

ISN'T THIS A LOVELY DAY

(To Be Caught in the Rain?)
from the RKO Radio Motion Picture TOP HAT

Words and Music by
IRVING BERLIN

Moderately slow Swing

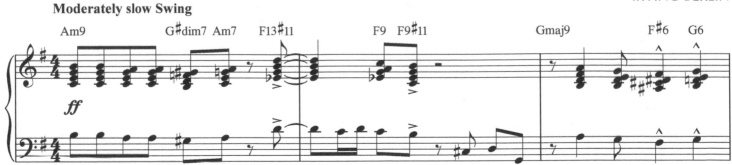

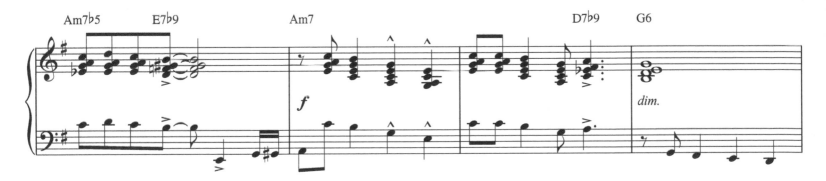

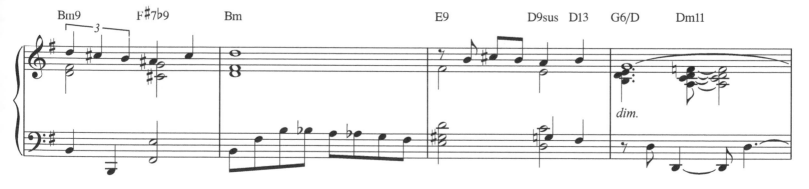

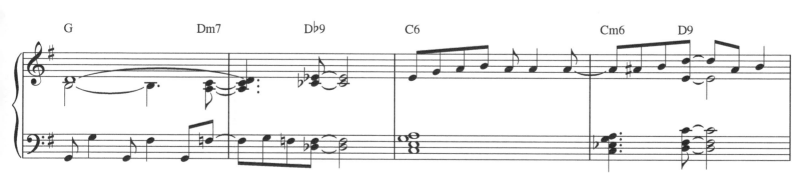

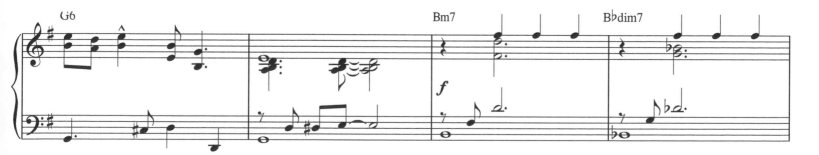

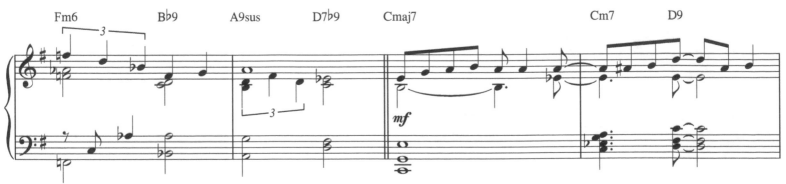

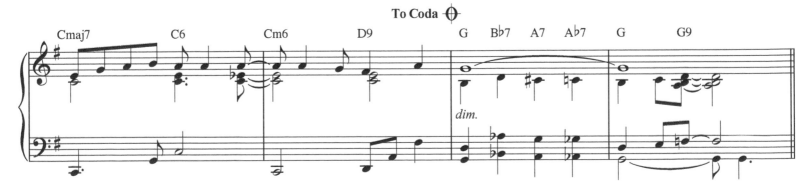

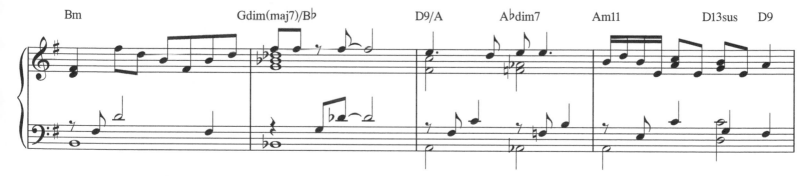

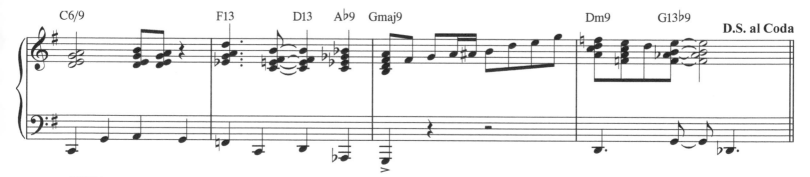

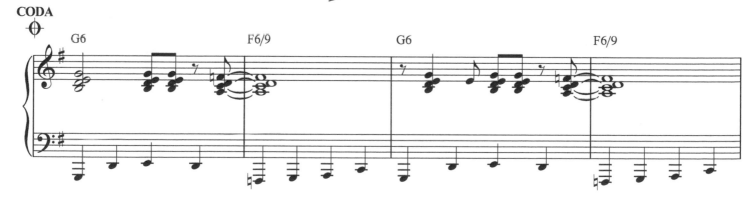

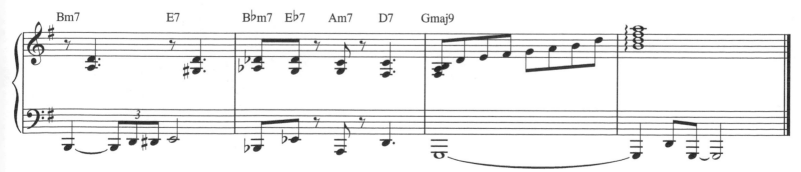

IT'S A LOVELY DAY TODAY

from the Stage Production CALL ME MADAM

Words and Music by
IRVING BERLIN

Moderate Swing

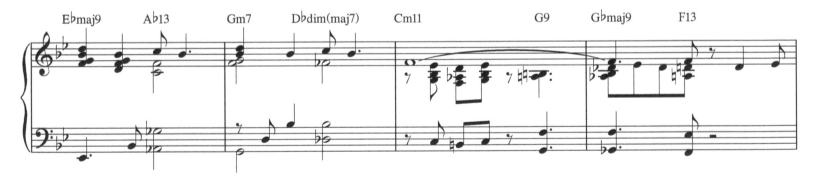

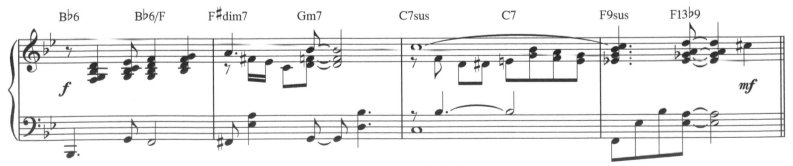

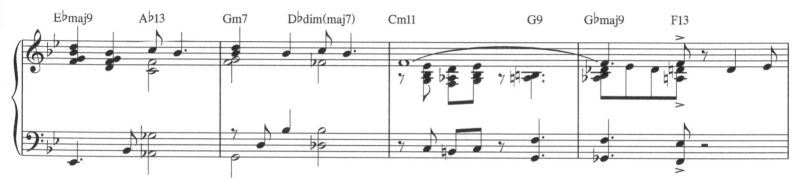

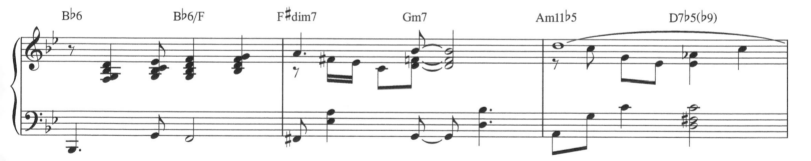

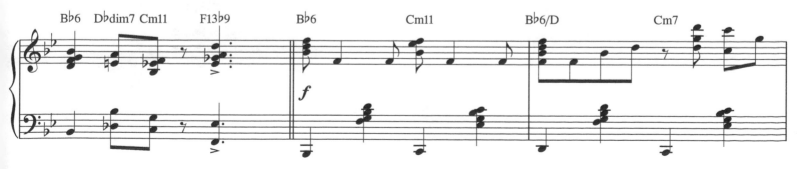

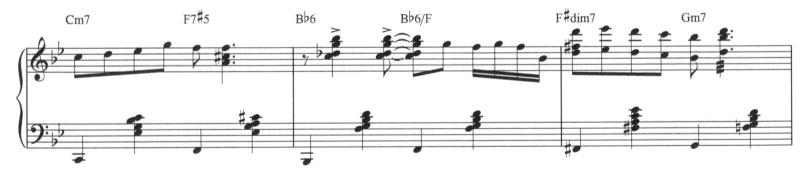

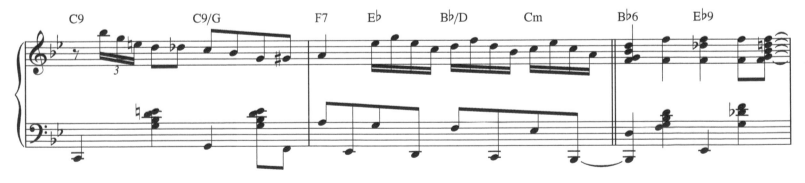

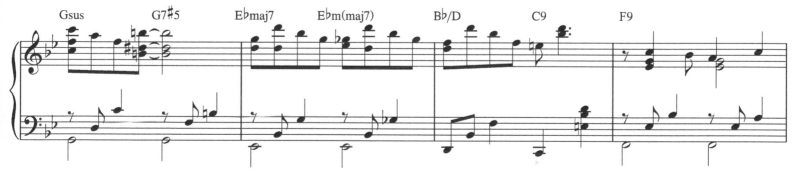

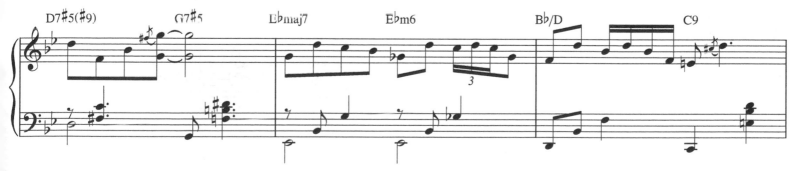

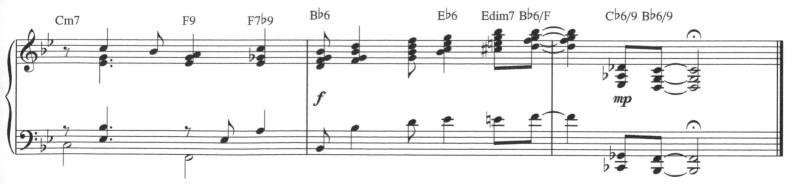

LET YOURSELF GO

from the Motion Picture FOLLOW THE FLEET

Words and Music by
IRVING BERLIN

Moderate Swing

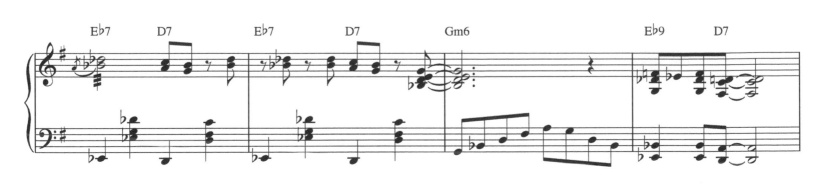

PUTTIN' ON THE RITZ

from the Motion Picture PUTTIN' ON THE RITZ

Words and Music by
IRVING BERLIN

Flowing, with rubato

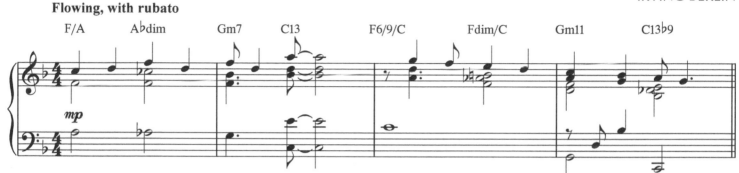

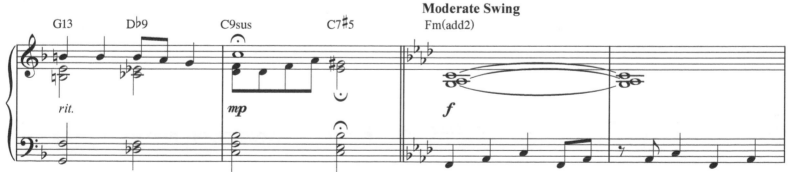

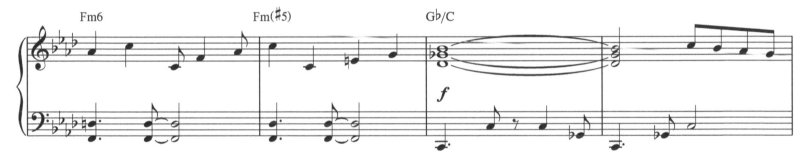

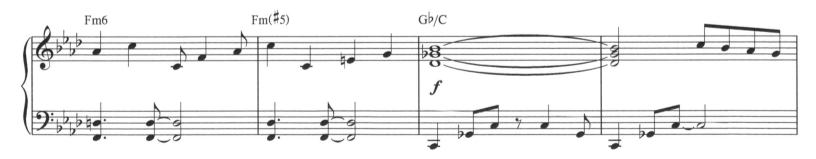

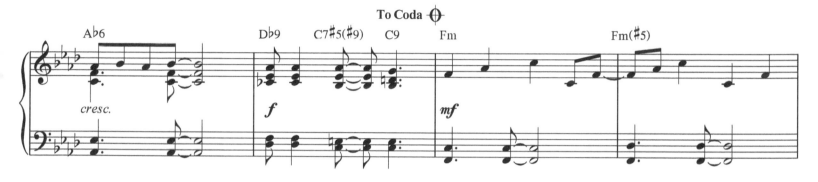

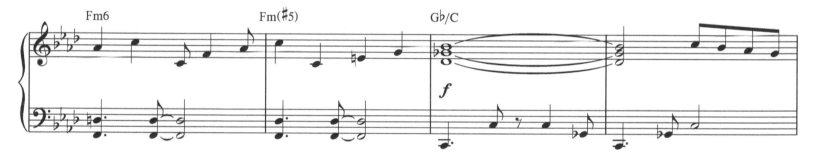

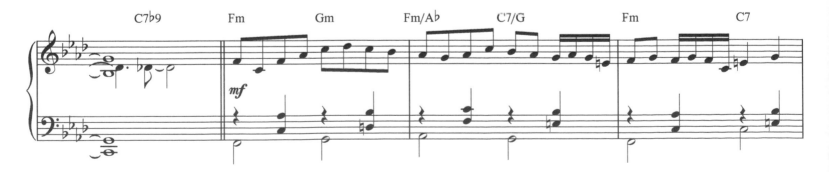

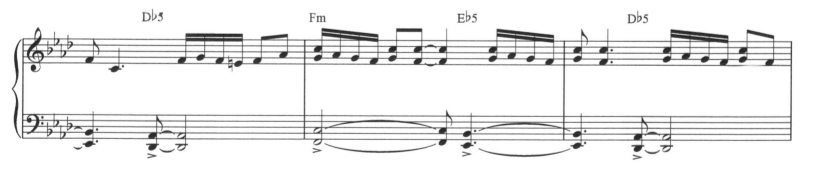

LET'S FACE THE MUSIC AND DANCE
from the Motion Picture FOLLOW THE FLEET

Words and Music by
IRVING BERLIN

Moderate Latin groove

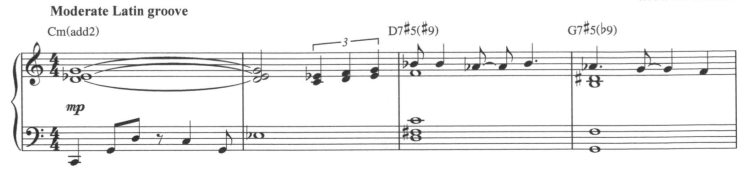

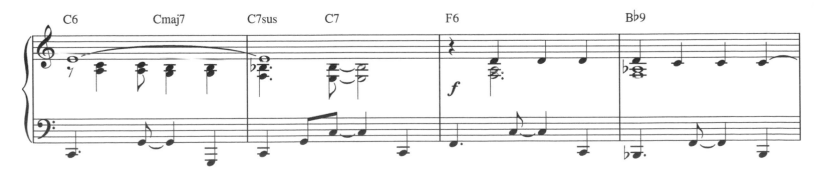

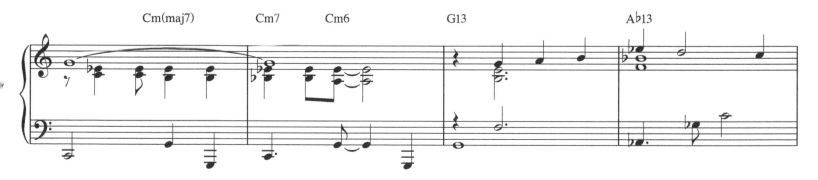

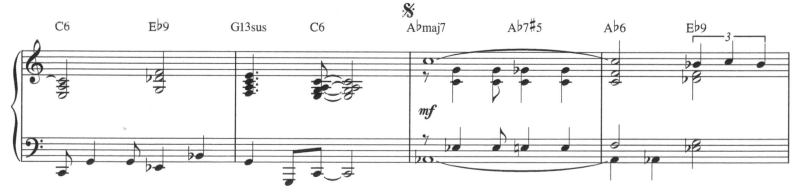

58

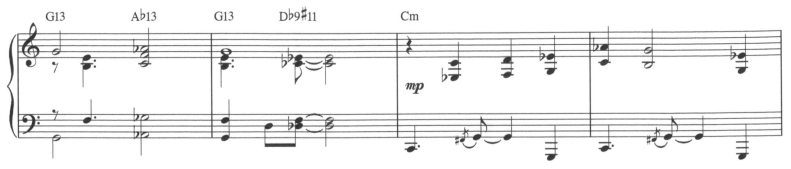

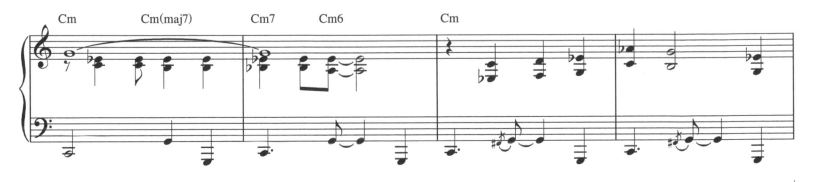

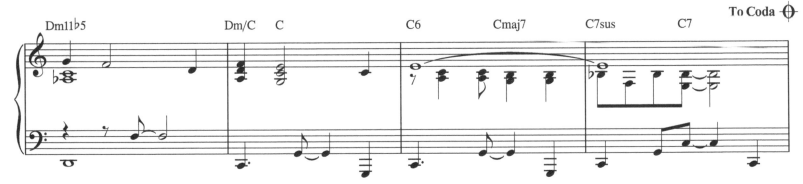

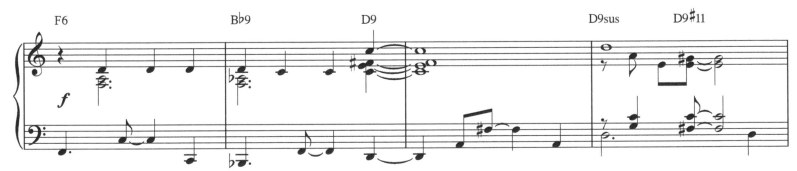

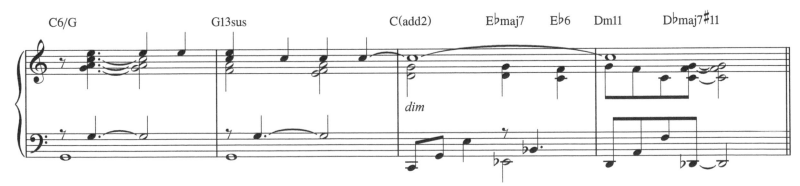

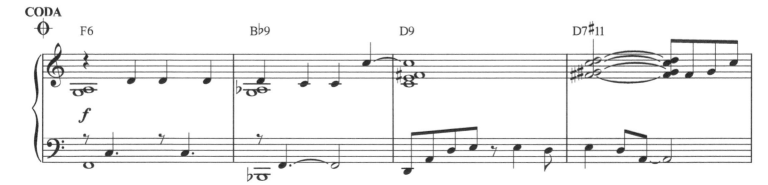

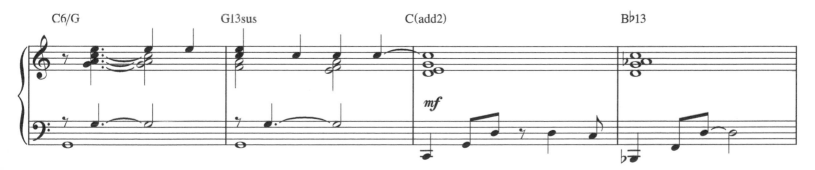

SAY IT ISN'T SO

Words and Music by
Irving Berlin

Bluesy Swing

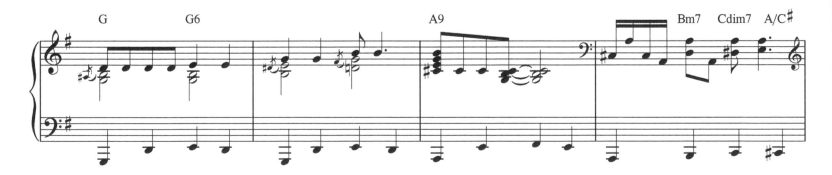

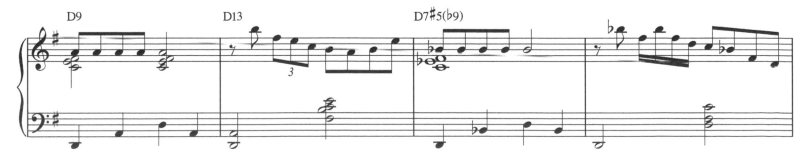

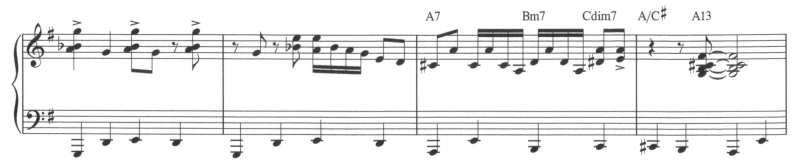

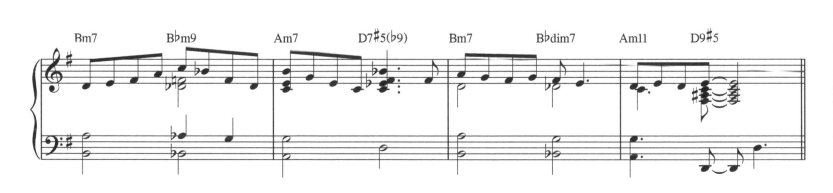

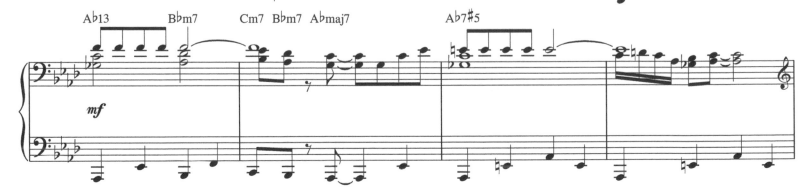

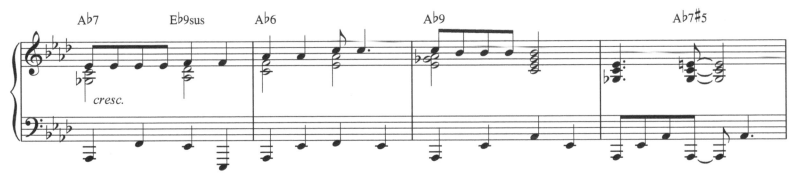

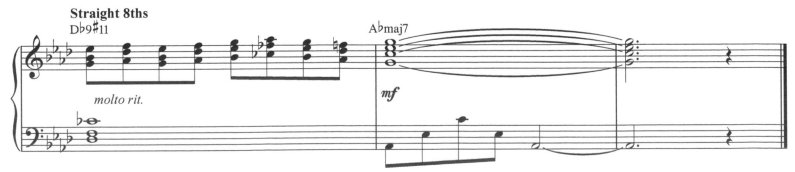

RUSSIAN LULLABY

Words and Music by
IRVING BERLIN

Moderate Waltz, straight 8ths

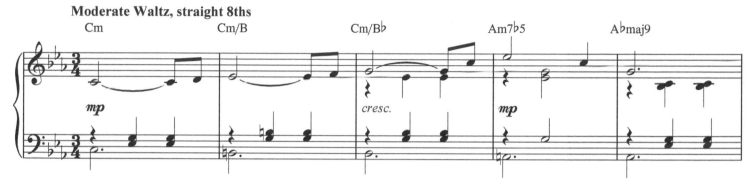

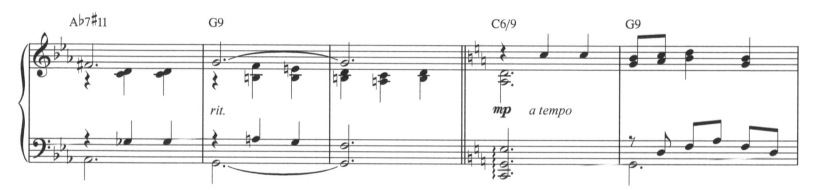

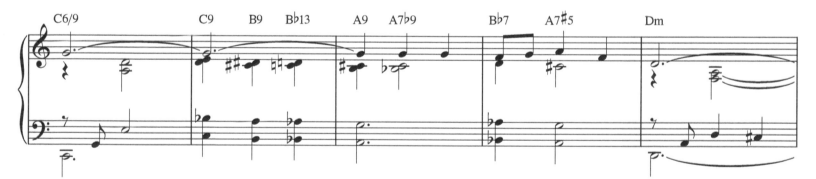

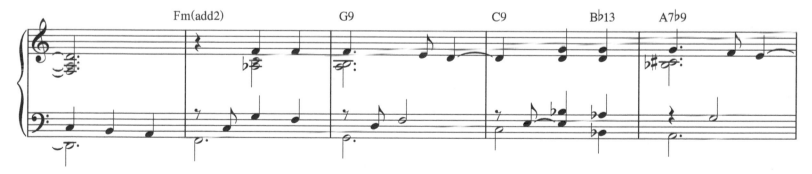

Moderate Swing

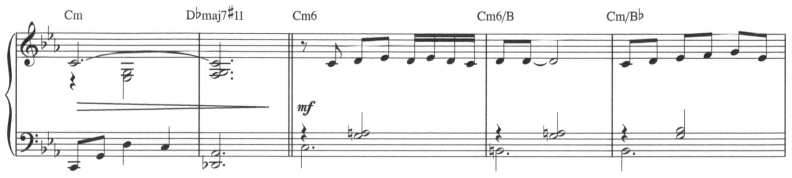

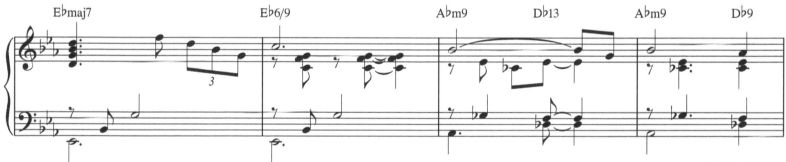

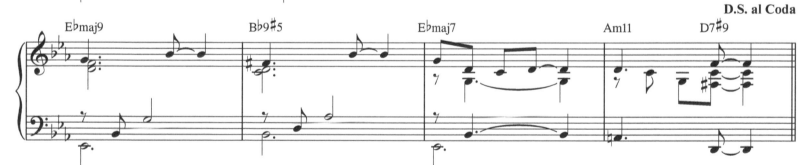

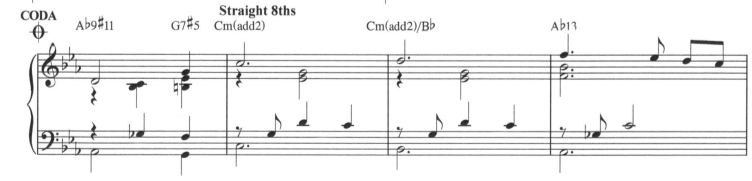

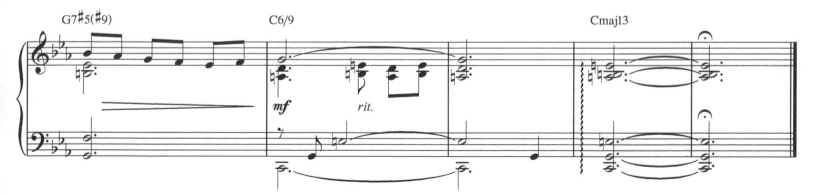

SAY IT WITH MUSIC
from the 1921 Stage Production MUSIC BOX REVUE

Words and Music by
IRVING BERLIN

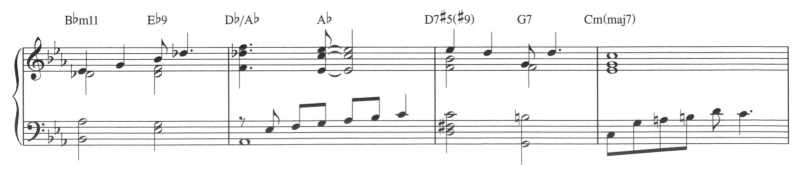

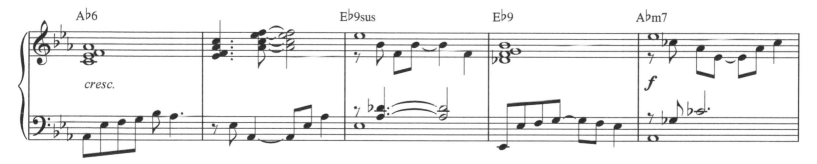

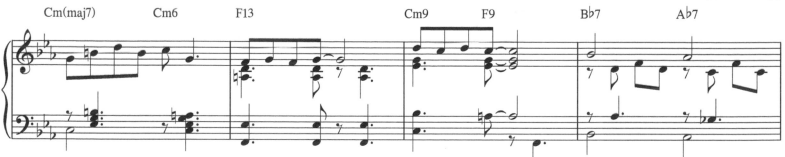

D.S. al Coda

CODA

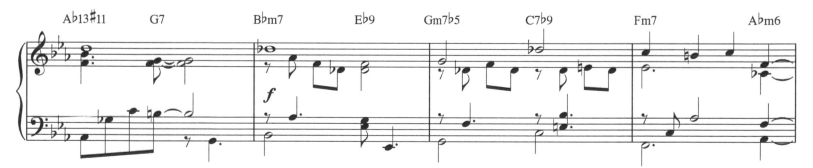

SOFT LIGHTS AND SWEET MUSIC

from the Stage Production FACE THE MUSIC

Words and Music by
IRVING BERLIN

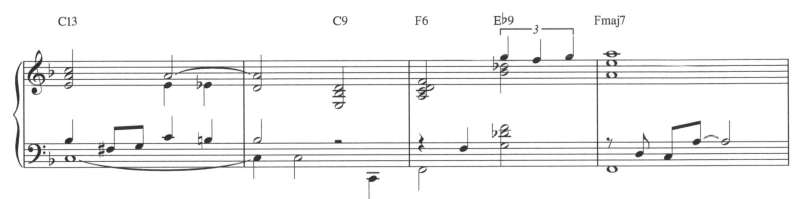

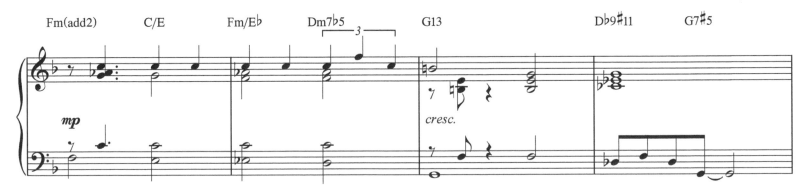

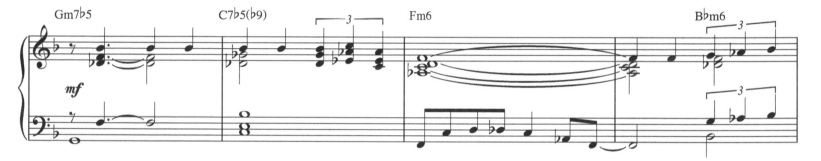

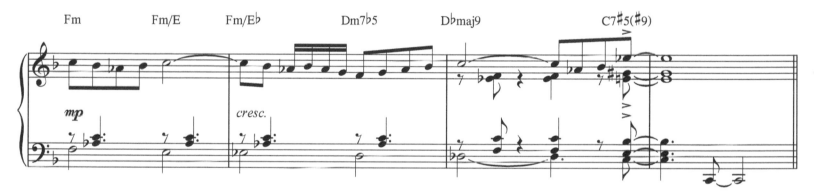

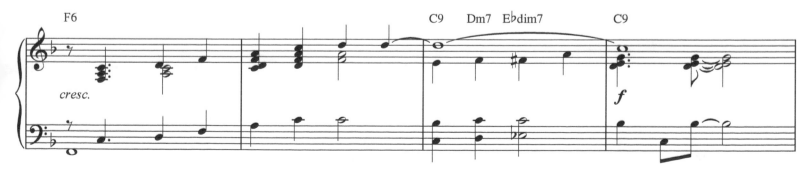

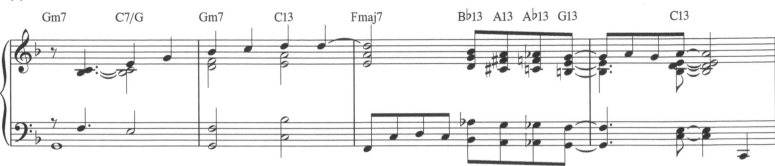

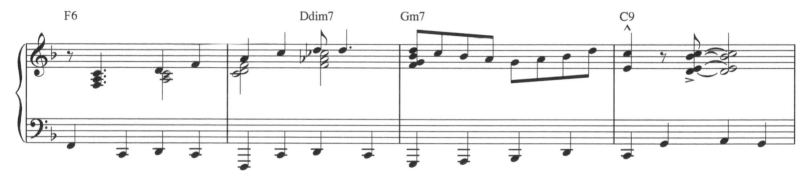

D.S. al Coda

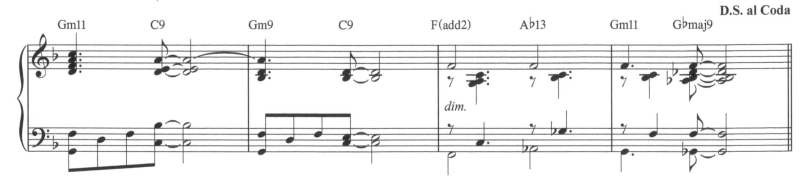

CODA

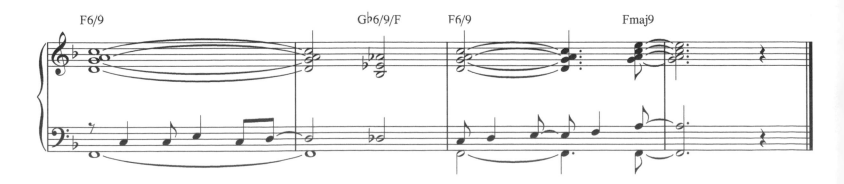

STEPPIN' OUT WITH MY BABY

from the Motion Picture Irving Berlin's EASTER PARADE

Words and Music by
IRVING BERLIN

Moderately slow Swing

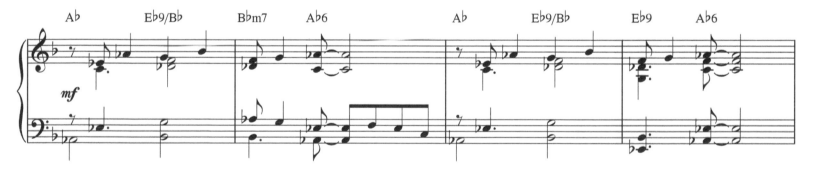

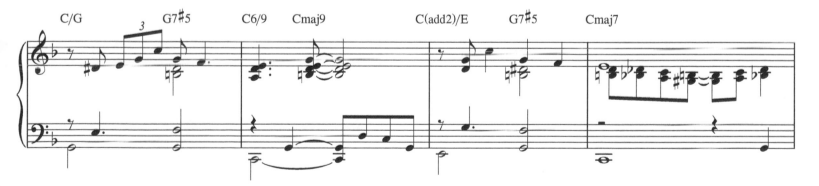

Medium jump tempo

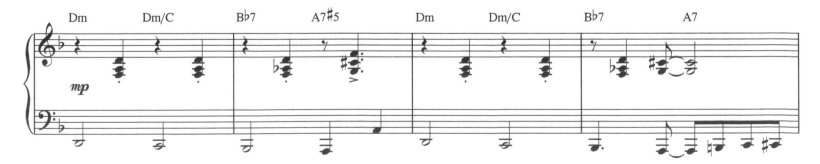

D.S. al Coda

CODA

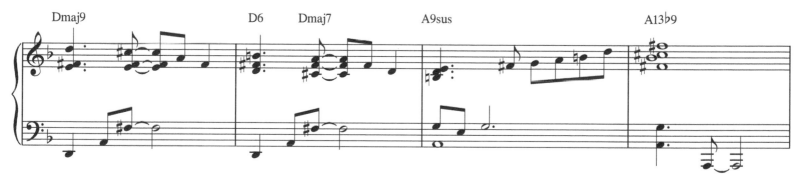

THE SONG IS ENDED
(But the Melody Lingers On)

Words and Music by
IRVING BERLIN

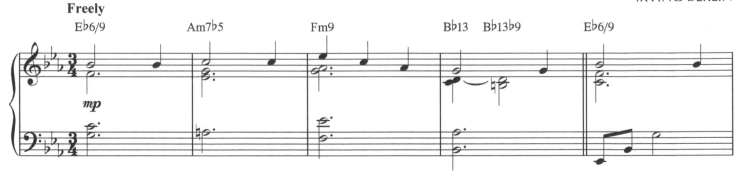

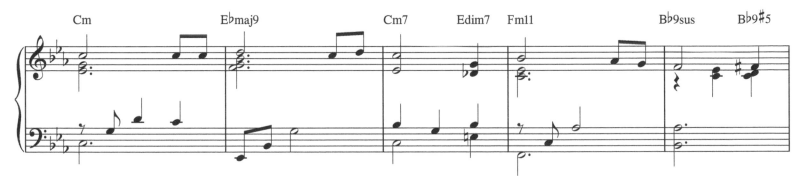

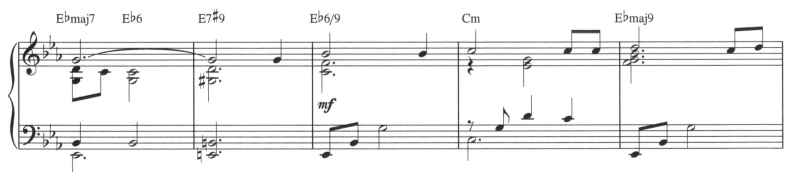

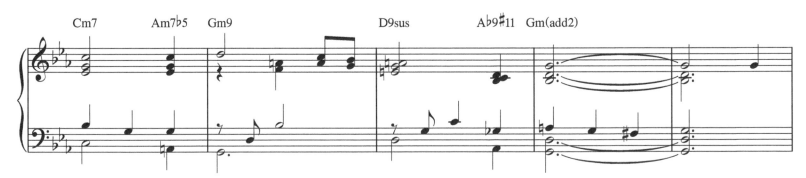

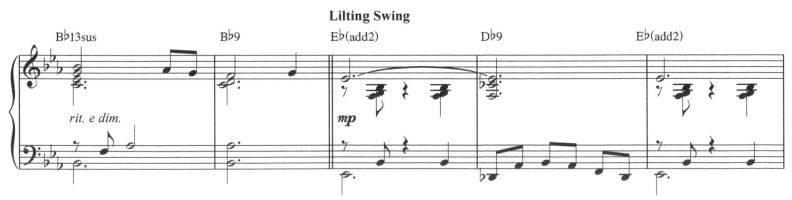

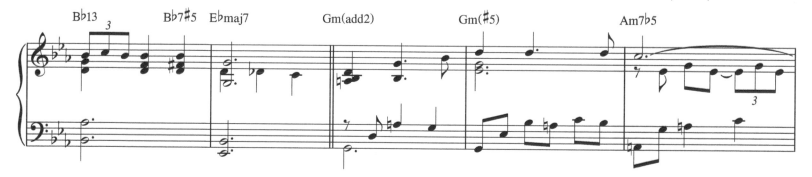

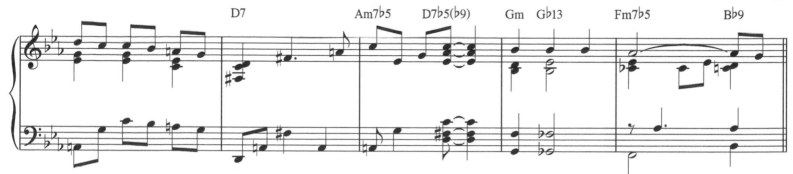

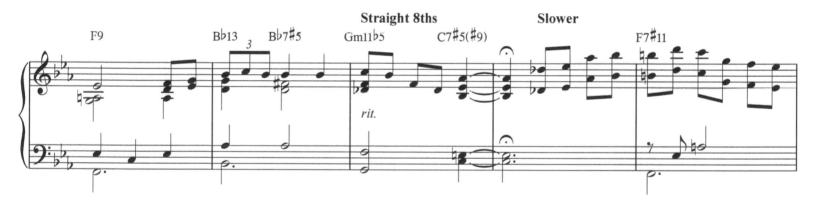

THEY SAY IT'S WONDERFUL

from the Stage Production ANNIE GET YOUR GUN

Words and Music by
IRVING BERLIN

Slow Swing

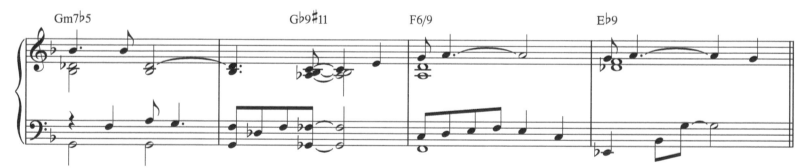

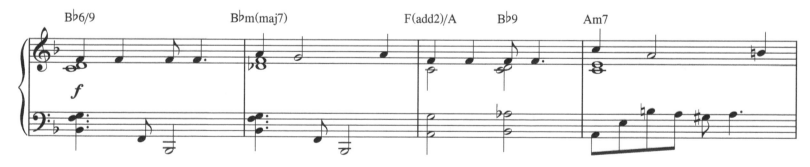

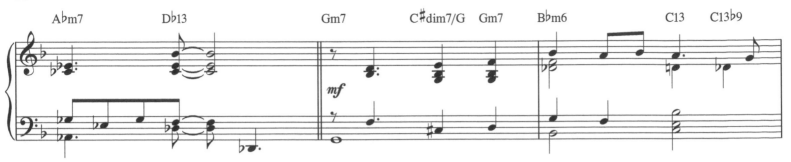

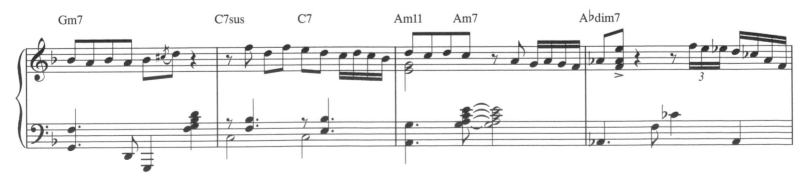

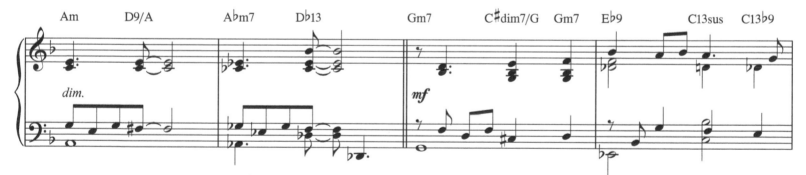

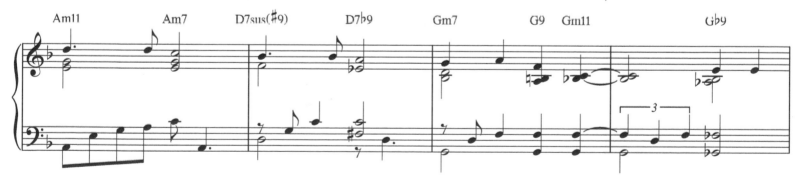

WHAT'LL I DO?
from MUSIC BOX REVUE OF 1924

Words and Music by
IRVING BERLIN

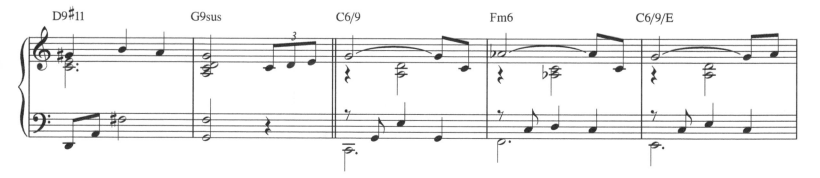

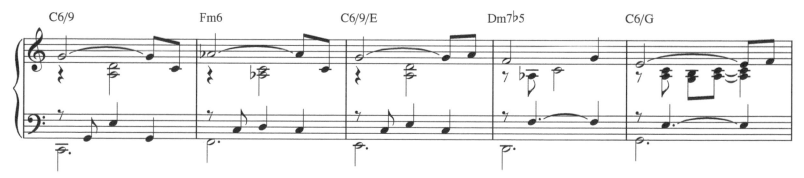

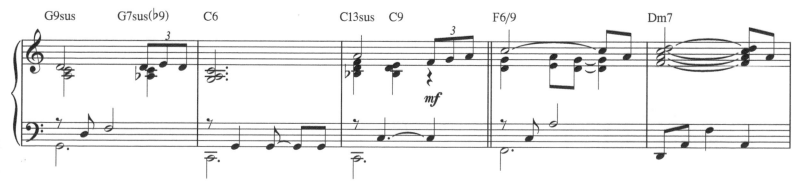

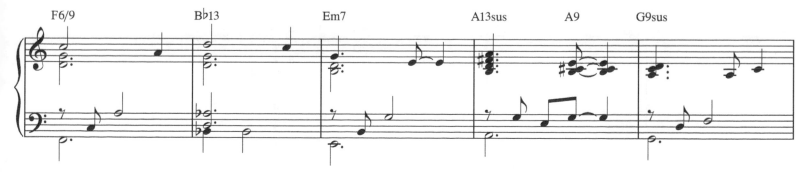

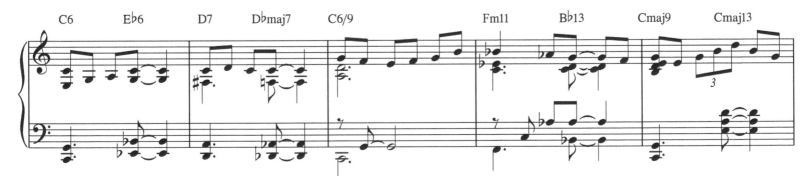

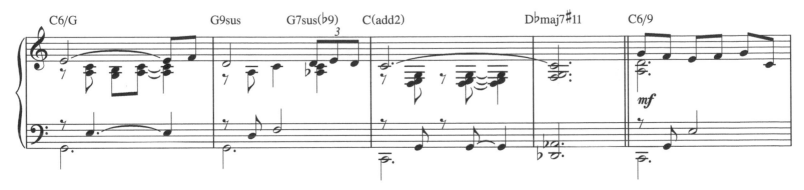

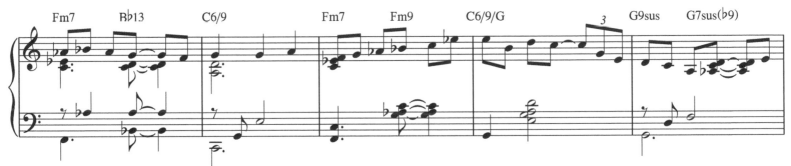

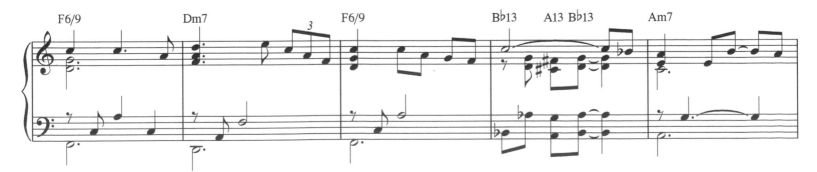

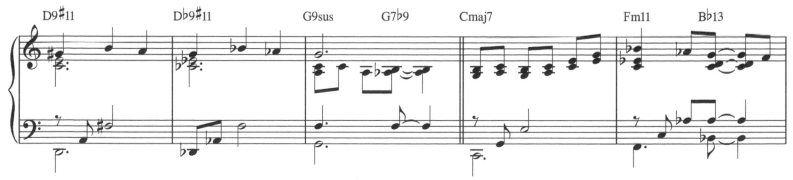

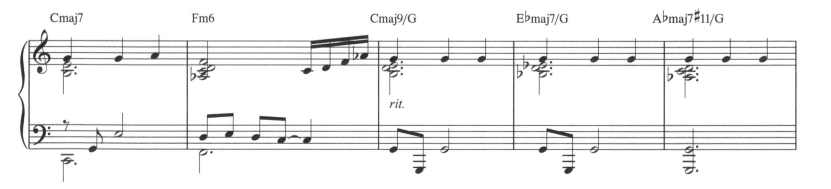

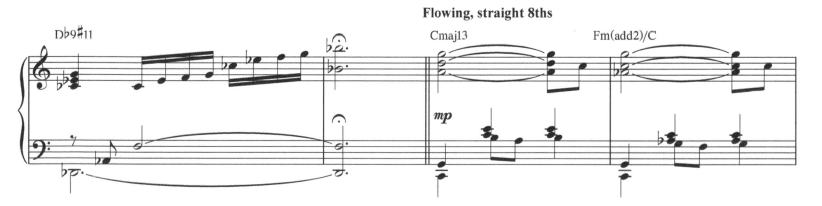

Flowing, straight 8ths

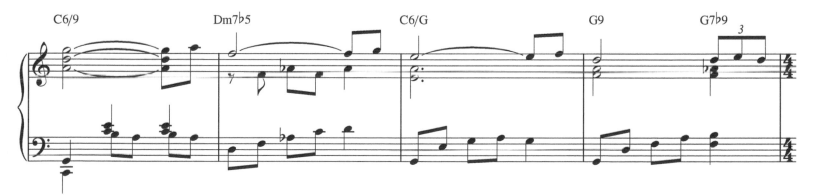

(I Wonder Why?)
YOU'RE JUST IN LOVE

from the Stage Production CALL ME MADAM

Words and Music by
IRVING BERLIN

Moderate Swing

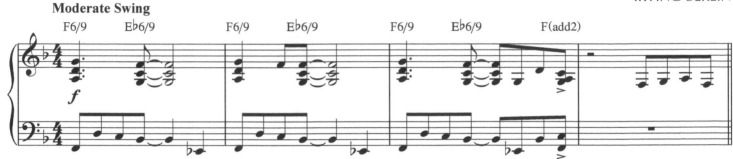

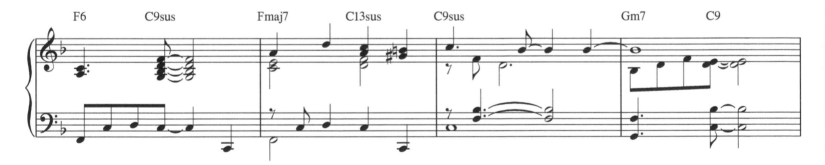

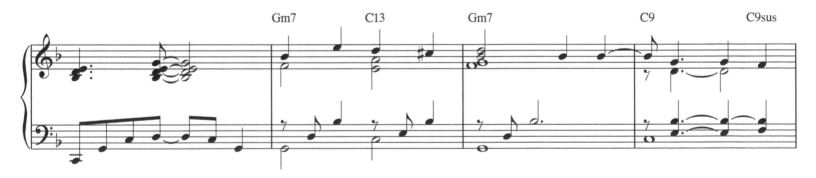

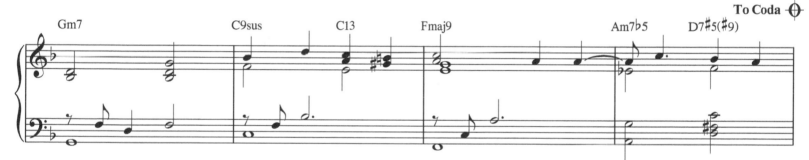

To Coda

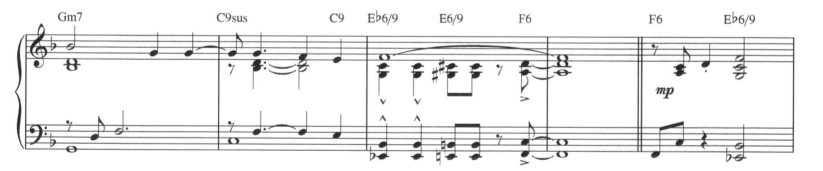

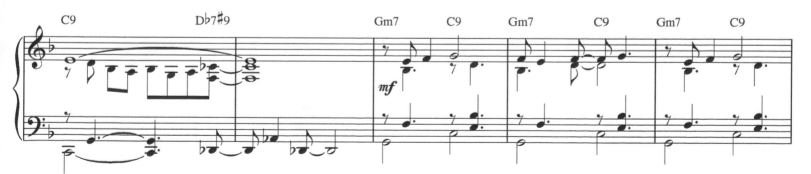

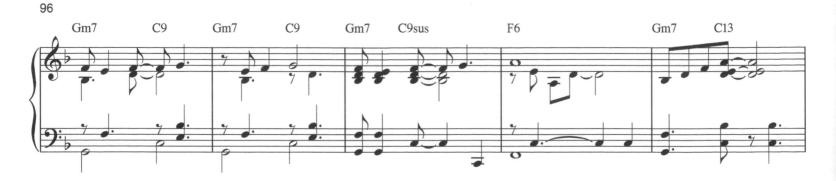

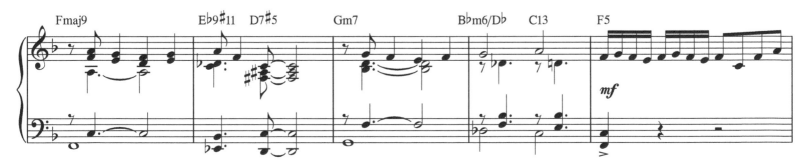

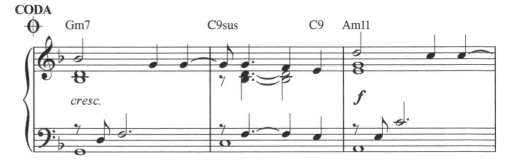

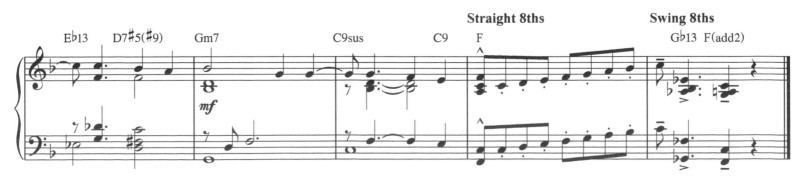